Lion Kings

Speedy Publishing LLC
40 E. Main St. #1156
Newark, DE 19711

www.speedypublishing.com

Copyright 2014
9781635014600
First Printed November 19, 2014

All Rights reserved. No part of this book may be reproduced or used in any way or form or by any means whether electronic or mechanical, this means that you cannot record or photocopy any material ideas or tips that are provided in this book.

Lion Facts...

The lion (Panthera leo) is one of the five big cats in the genus Panthera and a member of the family Felidae. With some males exceeding 250 kg (550 lb) in weight, it is the second-largest living cat after the tiger.

Lion Facts...

Wild lions currently exist in sub-Saharan Africa and in Asia (where an endangered remnant population resides in Gir Forest National Park in India) while other types of lions have disappeared from North Africa and Southwest Asia in historic times.

Lion Facts...

Until the late Pleistocene, about 10,000 years ago, the lion was the most widespread large land mammal after humans. They were found in most of Africa, across Eurasia from western Europe to India, and in the Americas from the Yukon to Peru.

Lion Facts...

The lion is a vulnerable species, having seen a major population decline in its African range of 30–50% per two decades during the second half of the 20th century.

Lion Facts...

Lion populations are untenable outside designated reserves and national parks. Although the cause of the decline is not fully understood, habitat loss and conflicts with humans are currently the greatest causes of concern. Within Africa, the West African lion population is particularly endangered.

Lion Facts...

Lions live for 10–14 years in the wild, while in captivity they can live longer than 20 years. In the wild, males seldom live longer than 10 years, as injuries sustained from continual fighting with rival males greatly reduce their longevity.

Lion Facts...

They typically inhabit savanna and grassland, although they may take to bush and forest. Lions are unusually social compared to other cats. A pride of lions consists of related females and offspring and a small number of adult males. Groups of female lions typically hunt together, preying mostly on large ungulates.

Lion Facts...

Lions are apex and keystone predators, although they are also expert scavengers obtaining over 50 percent of their food by scavenging as opportunity allows. While lions do not typically hunt humans, some have been known to do so.

Lion Facts...

Lioness will give birth to 1-3 cubs each 2 years. Cubs have spots at birth, but they disappear in time. After the first six weeks, the cubs are taken care of by all of the females and will often nurse from females other than their mother.

Lion Facts...

The roar of a lion can be heard from 8 kilometers (5.0 miles) away.

Lion Facts...

Lions can reach speeds of up to 81 kph (50 mph) but only in short bursts because of a lack of stamina.

Lion Facts...

Lionesses are better hunters than males and do most of the hunting for a pride.

Lion Facts...

In the wild, lions rest for around 20 hours a day.

Lion Facts...

Lions are easily recognized by their manes. Larger and darker mane suggests that lion is very strong and other lions often avoid him. Lionesses react differently – they are attracted by the large and dark manes.

Lion Facts...

When lion and lioness meet, they greet each other by rubbing. During this process, they exchange scents.

Lion Facts...

When young males reach maturity, older males will kick them out of the pride. When they wander on their own, young lions are known as nomads. If they manage to survive and gain strength, they will battle with other lions to take over a pride for themselves.

Lion Facts...

Lions have retractable claws, which mean that they could "hide" their claws during the play and avoid hurting each other.

Lion Facts...

When lion and tiger mate, new type of animal named liger is created. Liger has stripes like tiger, but the color of its fur is pale compared to tiger's fur.

Made in the USA
Middletown, DE
23 June 2019